LUMINARY VISION

LUMINARY VISION

Bruce Connolly

authorHOUSE®

AuthorHouse™
1663 Liberty Drive
Bloomington, IN 47403
www.authorhouse.com
Phone: 833-262-8899

Published by AuthorHouse 08/07/2023

ISBN: 979-8-8230-1228-7 (sc)
ISBN: 979-8-8230-1227-0 (e)

Library of Congress Control Number: 2023913798

Print information available on the last page.

CONTENTS

LAUNCH OF PEACE AND FREEDOM

HAND
OUT
AND
Up

SOLID

LAUNCH OF PEACE AND FREEDOM

My first book of this enlightenment series discussed the Dimensions of the Mind, Body, Soul, Spirit, and Universe and how terrorization brings a person their family, community, country and world out of harmony and balance and how harmony and balance was returned to a person and their family, community, country and world when their terrorization end.

My second book of this enlightenment series discussed the Espionage of the Lord God Almighty, Jesus, Holy Spirits and We The People, how the criminal terrorists use the Devils vessel of offenses, known as the Arc of the Covenant (the breach of the Covenant of the Lord God Almighty and humanity), games, lies and deceit to criminally assault in psychological warfare and physical warfare the Lord God Almighty flocks of the Lord God Almighty and Jesus by violating their laws and rules to often validate the criminal assaults. These are criminal assaults in war and are one hundred percent wrong, there is no excuse for these war crimes. The book goes on to discuss how Peace and Freedom was achieved on all of the Lord God Almighty planets including the Earth.

Used throughout this book the word exploitation, the definition:

to treat yourself or someone else unfairly. Some people may even think it's a benefit to you and them to exploit someone, usually the toxic people of humanity have these thoughts.

This being the third book of enlightenment will discuss what the luminary vision is like for We The People with the launching of Peace and Freedom. Living in Peace is Freedom of disturbance and living in security, tranquility in law and order and truth. Living in freedom is the right to act, speak as one without hindrance or restraint by any other person or governing authority. Living in Peace and Freedom is a God given right and entitlement to all human beings until they are proven to be a criminal, either in society or war, they then can be incarcerated and held in a prison for a sentenced amount of time. The criminals lose their right and entitlement as Devils or human beings to be free. Now that the Manowar and the Vortex of Protection have been presented to all human beings on all of the Lord God Almighty planets and governments to end all Holy wars, including Extreme Nazi wars of slavery and/or mental slavery, Nazi wars and all other wars known to humankind, that are psychological warfare and physical warfare for a great resolve of Peace and Freedom. This would virtually protect all humanity from ongoing threats of domestic and/or foreign terrorism, including slavery and/or mental slavery sponsored by any governance, community or group. These hate crimes of humanity would be defended on an ongoing basis. Both the Manowar protection for humanity and the Vortex of Protection are mandates for all human beings, all governments, all judicial systems on all of the Lord God Almighty planets including the Earth. This would also end the Devils game of the Devils and human beings that is synonymous with wars, a game, is just a horrendous way of describing a war.

This landing of all of humanity on all of the Lord God Almighty planets may not have been ideal, but the landing was halted before bottoming out on all of the planets including the Earth. These offenses and progressive offenses were spiraling out of control on all of the Lord God Almighty planets, in all galaxies to the bitter end of all people on each planet, including the Earth. The progressive defense, defending all humanity from any and all offenses of the Devils and humanity and progressive offenses of the Devils and humanity. By protecting and defending humanity from intentional offensive crimes and/or intentional errors in judgment of offensive crimes regardless of the justification for these offensive crimes, including slavery and/or mental slavery is the solution to the offensive crime in war problems in our generation and all future generations to come. This gives all humanity and the planets a new launch point for beautiful happenings to bloom and rise.

No longer will a criminal offense in war, of people be considered a defense of people. Forever and always heinous crimes of humanity.

This protects and defends all humanity for the Passion of Christ, Covenants, Virtues and Values to be available to all human beings on all of the Lord God Almighty planets. The true Passion of You could now come to fruition with the Passion of Christ, Covenants, Virtues, Values and the Interests you can now develop as a person!

Life by people in society is much, much more respectful between people in families and outside of families in communities and between societies. Rather than hidden actions behind lies and deceit actions are justified for truths within governments. Trust shines through with this respect, values and truthfulness. Loyalty builds in families, communities, between communities, within countries and between countries and within worlds and between worlds. People become more helpful, courteous and kind to others and even within yourself. A reverence becomes apparent for God and your country. People become more cheerful, happy and confident with themselves and others. There is a friendliness that emanates from you and each person living in Peace and Freedom.

There is a serenity among people in Peace and Freedom where dreams are very much more achievable, a more completeness within a person and a family, a community and a country. Goals for the people and the society are also much more achievable, personal, professional, vocational, trade and volunteer including technical to advance quicker and more proficiently.

In Peace and Freedom the people can worship the Passion of the

3

Lord, Passion of Jesus and together the Passion of Christ and be in harmony and balance with their dimensions of the mind, body, soul, spirit and universe. This will bring the preponderance of families together and united, communities together and united, countries together and united and worlds together and united. United we Stand, Divided we fall! In the horror of war and slavery we crumble and fall!

This Gift of Peace and Freedom comes from Heaven, at the top rung of the ladder and above the top rung of the ladder itself for all human beings on all of the Lord God Almighty planets including the Earth, right next to the Passion of Christ themselves, to protect and serve all human beings from the horrors of psychological warfare and physical warfare. A life virtually free of criminal war, domestic terrorism and foreign terrorism and physical and mental slavery.

The **ladder of truth** is as follows, going up for truth:

Embracement of one another as people, greatness and beauty, great leaders, justice, law enforcement

Acceptance of one another as people, greatness, and glimmers of beauty, leaders, justice, law enforcement

Indifference of one another as people, however tolerance

Non Acceptance of one another as people, hate criminals, war criminals, terrorists of humanity domestically or foreign, the offenders can be devils or people, the predominant liars of humanity, very sociopathic in nature, very toxic to most other people, even themselves, the dark evil of humanity.

Going up the **ladder of truth** leads to constructive societies and worlds, the good holy of humanity, going down the ladder of truth leads to the destruction of societies and worlds. The new progressive protection/defense of the Lord God Almighty and the Manowar with the Vortex of Protection is for all humanity except for the toxic Devils and humans in war with their offense and progressive offense, this will protect the rest of humanity from the majority of war and slavery and/or mental slavery assaults by the toxic offenders of humanity. The toxic offenders in war of all people from the bottom rung of the ladder through the top rung of the ladder would be given a choice to surrender for Peace and Freedom or be executed to death, capital punishment for their capital crimes of humanity, held as prisoners of war. The toxic people may be too demented and deranged mindfully to coexist with humanity without being incarcerated. Toxic people at war are weapons of mass destruction too dangerous to remain free, offending from the Devil's vessel of Dark/Evil, known as the Arc of the Covenant (the breach of the Covenant of the Lord God Almighty and humanity). The same is true with slave masters as weapons of mass destruction; they are too dangerous to remain free as well. And calling war slavery and/or mental slavery a game is just a crying shame by a mentally demented and deranged people, who assaults, enslaves and murders other people and the masses of people for sport, the same as the Devil's game, offending from the Devil's vessel, the Arc of the Covenant of Dark/Evil.

The criminals of humanity offend from the vessel of the Arc of Covenant of Dark/Evil and Lies and Deceit often games and trickery of the Devils to harm, murder, and extort from humanity and in some cases in doing so, enslave and/or mentally enslave humanity illegally, always optional/unnecessary assaults of humanity. The Protectors/Defenders of humanity try to solve the riddle of the vessel the Arc of Covenant of the Dark/Evil of humanity with the vessel of Truth of the Covenant of Christ, Virtues, Values and Interests always required/necessary in humanity for justice and to serve and protect the people from the Dark/Evil assaults.

The Devils of humanity and the line of people that are toxic offenders are always wrong for any and all societies. The power and control of any community, country or world is absolutely devastating. Left in power and control they would end all humanity in uncontrollable heinous crimes leading to devastating abomination of events on any planet they exist on and left in power and control for an extended period of time. This protection system will right the wrong of having the toxic offenders of humanity in power and control of their communities, countries or world now and ongoing.

Life would no longer be led in predominant worry and fear of being a war casualty mentally or physically. There would be fewer criminals in society and worry and fear from these criminals would also subside. The brave and true would now shine and be able to stand as champions and heroes of their countries and worlds!

These criminal syndicates of the governments or worlds would no longer be able to control societies as toxic hate racketeering, torcherous, enslavement and murderous criminals in domestic or foreign terrorism in wars or games as they are also considered wars!

Reality of Peace
As we search for peace, within and around,
It will appear and become more than just a vision, and a dream,
It will come to life inside, and about us,
The fire that destroyed, will now burn to light,
It will dance within us, and about us,
More than a vision and a dream, a realization,
For all to experience, each one and bound,
Intertwined in reality, and self guidance!

Reality of Freedom
When freedom rings in, with liberty in the air,
There is a certain tone, within each note,
That catch's, and cannot be caught,
We can think and move, without a care,
The spark to light our fire,
Can no longer be extinguished, from our desires,
The flame of truth will ever grow high,
Within us all, as we stand tall and fair!

VORTEX
OF
REPAIRATION

VORTEX OF REPAIRATION

Shortly after the Manowar defended the universes from the onslaught of the Devils the Manowar then started the build of the Vortex of Protection, and almost synonymously started the build of a Vortex of Repairation. The Vortex of Repairation is also a mandate for all human beings, all governments, all judicial systems on all of the Lord God Almighty planets including the Earth. Hiding the Vortex of Protection and/or the Vortex of Repairation to any and all humanity is a war crime, government secrecy and confidentiality won't stop the presentation of these to all humanity on any or all planets including the Earth. Also overriding the laws and rules of Vortex of Protection and/or Vortex of Repairation by any of humanity on any planet, government and or justice system is illegal and a war crime including the Earth.

The Vortex of Repairation is for the Passion of Christ with the Manowar to help humanity help themselves with the damage caused mentally in the horrors of psychological warfare and/or physical warfare.

Some of the reparations the Manowar put up into the Vortex of Repairation was to help with religious bigotry, racial bigotry, culture bigotry, gender bigotry, law and order and justice bigotry not for indifference, but to repair from hatred, if the people are open and can be helped. Help with mental bipolar, schizophrenia, anxiety, dementia, alzheimer assaults done in war with reparations if the people are open and can be helped. Put up into the Vortex of Repairation help for drug and alcohol exploitation legal or illegal of the person with the problem, if they are willing to get help. Societies in both psychological warfare and physical warfare lean on drugs and alcohol to medicate, many out of control. Put up into the Vortex of Repairation grief help from the many losses incurred in war, war is full of grief and loss. This help is also directed at professional, vocational and technical experts including all of the people damaged in war to aid the people with their anguish and counseling needs within the governments and in the private sectors to achieve better mental and physical health.

To aid with these reparations of humanity the Manowar also put up Respect, Faith, Love, Hope, Belief, Compassion, Grace, Mercy, Forgiveness, Caring, Empathy, Unity, the Passion of the Lord God Almighty, the Passion of Jesus, the Passion of Christ, the Passion of the Holy Spirits and more...

The Lord God Almighty, Jesus, Holy Spirits can if they wish add to the Vortex Of Repairation as needed. They will aid with the reparation of humanity from the Vortex of Repairation with their ultimate supreme divine power.

The Manowar put up into the Vortex of Repairation for humanity to come together and not only repair the damage done to planets but to reverse the damage done to planets by human exploitation. Damage done to our air quality, water quality, ground coverage and wildlife.

Much of the damage to humanity that needs repair has been through bigotry. This was done by the wrong side of war being supremacists and holding other races or religions, cultures, peace officers of lesser value than theirs, the hate crimes of humanity. Treating them very poorly when they should be treated equally at all times. This is the acceptance we must fix and equalize in our societies to live in equal Peace and Freedom. This includes the war between genders when one gender feels supreme over another. We must put the bigotry slurs aside and come to an equalization. To lean into each other for a common health, wealth and wisdom and well being of all people.

When we fail to do this we lean more on the exploitation of alcohol and both illegal and legal drugs for support. We should be leaning on each other for support, not ill advised vices.

A lot of bigotry is begot through the exploitation of people of races, religions, cultures and territorial supremacy and dominance over other races and religions done through wars of humankind. This same kind of exploitation and dominance of people can happen with genders of humanity also remnants of wars or conflicts of humanity. This same type of bigotry can happen with crime syndicates and gangs in cities and countries and syndicates in governments for supremacy and dominance over territory and humanity for exploitation rites, also hate crimes.

If we can learn that this exploitation of humanity, alcohol, drugs and weapons brings society out of harmony and balance and into a very aggressive and destructive nature and hence reverse this exploitation, society is much better off. By education of those involved with these exploitations of people, and teaching more passively and assertively with more counseling how the Covenants of the Passion of Christ come into a person's life, virtues come into a person's life, values can come into a person's life, interests can come into a person's life and dimensions of the mind, body, soul, spirit, and universe can come into a person's life a life changing experience can happen, we have a more constructive experience!

If the offenders of humanity can learn how to reconcile their differences passively and/or assertively then the defensive party can also interact passively and/or assertively and does not have to take a defensive aggressive posture! An offensive aggressive posture usually brings out a poor resolution in a conflict where people get injured or killed! The offensive aggressive posture is not required or necessary, is optional and the defensive aggressive posture may be required to resolve the conflict and injury is often the result.

Many of the offenders of humanity emotions run rampant in anger, discontent and frustration at not getting their desired goal through good negotiation, ambassador and communication skills. If a mediator and/or counselor can be called in to help resolve the problems and issues to a peaceful resolution it is always for the best! These are natural human emotions in all of us that are rooted more deeply in some than others. Somehow where these human emotions run that deep they must be identified and dealt with in people by mental health professionals before an uncontrollable offensive criminal action occurs. Terroristic wars, domestic assaults, mass shootings, road rage, etc..., these offenses occur. Conflict intervention, counseling and education is the key to halting offenses and repeat offenses, the mindful approach!

Reparations from these wars of humanity can occur and bigotry of races, religions, cultures and genders can move beyond chaos and violence, and tolerance and even to acceptance and embracement of one another in society can happen to live in Peace and Freedom with the proper counseling and education in our societies, the more mindful approach!

How does the Vortex of Repairation work in helping peoples losses in psychological warfare and physical warfare? The divine power descends from above to give people strength in a togetherness to a common end for the good and gain of all, a shroud of Holy aid. This gives the champion and heroes of all countries people to come to the aid of those in need. Those in need an openness to receive the proper reparation, if possibly in their mind's eye. Brings people together, united to stand and help each other. United we all stand and succeed, divided those will fall and fail. This will work as the casualties of war will be healed as well as everyday life of society in Peace and Freedom.

Offensive aggression usually happens with pent up anger and frustration emotional issues that all humans have. However, in some people these emotional issues become uncontrollable to cause human harm and murder to other human beings and destruction of human possessions. Offensive aggression is always an optional way to settle differences between people. Passive and assertive communication is the correct approach in all interactions.

The defense aggression of offensive aggression is automatic in many human beings. It's the flight and fight response.

If aggressive defenses need to be built, they should be done in a simulation mode, not involving humans or pets in harm, enslavement or murder, an abomination of humankind. This could be done as maneuvers, computer simulation and contact sports such as boxing and martial arts where danger and harm can be minimal. Human beings and pets should not be used as live guinea pigs for offensive warfare fodder.

When real people are harmed by the criminals of humanity, war or otherwise they can possibly get forgiveness through the pond of redemption to aid in their reparation. This is through the Passion of Christ with the Beast of the Lord God Almighty, although this forgiveness of sins varies in many religions. Usually this involves asking the Passion of Christ, Jesus and/or the Lord God Almighty through your religious leaders for forgiveness for your crimes/sins with prayers, apologizing to those you harmed if possible, community service, and maybe even financial retribution. This goes a long way toward the reparation of a person's mind, body, soul and spirit and universe.

The **ladder of truth** in reparation is as follows, going up for truth:

Embracement of one another as people, greatness and beauty

Acceptance of one another as people, greatness, glimmers of beauty

Indifference of one another as people, however tolerance

Non Acceptance of one another as people, hate criminals, war criminals, terrorists of humanity domestically or foreign, the offenders can be devils or people, the predominant liars of humanity, very sociopathic in nature, very toxic to most other people, including themselves, the dark evil of humanity.

More people will be going up the **ladder of truth** leading to constructive societies and worlds, the good holy of humanity, rather than going down the ladder of truth leading to the destruction of societies and worlds. This will happen very quickly once all wars are brought to an end and humanity is living in Peace and Freedom.

Footprint to Recovery
There may not be a exact footprint to recovery,
But we the many attempt to invent one,
Most care,
And always try,
It's the love within us, that makes us that wise,
To go on for the best,
To go forward,
Without stepping on each others feet,
We keep on moving forward,
Always believing,
In us, the Holy Father, Son, Holy Spirits and all our Holy Ones
Forever we speak!

OUTLOOK
FOR
PLANETS

GOVERNMENT

SUN

EARTH

<u>INNOVATION</u> - SOLAR, WIND, POWER

HYDROLOGY

ENVIORNMENT

AGRICULTURE   FORESTRY

EDUCATION   MEDICAL THERAPY

CARE   <u>SUPPORT</u> - BACKBONE

OUTLOOK FOR PLANETS

Utilize already known solar resources, wind resources and ocean wave, lake wave, and river power resources that are cleaner rather than the non-renewable resources such as our fossil fuels and their derivatives around the entire planet including the Earth. Reduce our carbon footprint that has such a horrendous short term and long term effect on our environment and ecology, including a detrimental effect on our weather. Possibly magnifying the solar input to get more energy production from each panel through a process of magnifying and mirroring that may be more productive. Increasing the turbine's differential to gather more energy from each wind turbine.

Electric transportation should be the goal around the planet, not just selected countries. Enrich freeways and highways to an electric grid to automatically maneuver vehicle transportation across nations within the world. More proficiently with fewer accidents being the goal.

Expand our rail system to above ground level monorail systems with both above ground and ground level stations for people's convenience. These could be in all weather climates and flood zones. Monorails could also be utilized for product transportation delivery services in many cases. Product and passenger monorails could even be on different lines.

For ecosystem and climate purposes replenish our rainforests through good forestry stewardship programs on every continent where applicable around the planet. On the Earth replenish the rainforests for certain in South America and Africa continents. Also for ecosystem and climate purposes through good stewardship programs replenish all forests that can be reasonably done around the planet, for climate, for wildlife and us.

Establish rain gardens or likeness in our urban, suburban and rural communities to protect our water resources from pollutants. These could be designed in urban, suburban and rural towns with both beauty and use in mind and the rural agriculture land primarily the use for filtering pollutants and protecting the agriculture land including orchard agricultural lands from soil erosion around the planet. All watershed districts should be studied for soil erosion impact and rain garden potential, this includes oceans, lakes, rivers and creeks. These would also be for the stewardship of our wildlife resources in each designated property. Continue the use of agricultural windbreaks for soil erosion control, beauty and wildlife preservation purposes.

Establish more hydroponic gardens for personal use and in communities for organic gardening. These hydroponic gardens could be more commercialized along water resources, including oceans, where the ocean water could be filtered from sodium for a lower or no sodium water content and could be used for growing edible plants.

Expand programs for disposing of hazardous chemicals from the more advanced countries around the globe to lesser developed countries.

Expand programs for disposing human waste from the more advanced countries around the globe to lesser developed countries.

As is done in many communities, establish waste programs for yard, organic, recyclable and garbage waste in every community around the planet.

Filter our oceans and lakes for garbage deposits from the past and recycle the garbage that can be recycled properly and dispose of the remaining garbage properly.

Utilize recycled materials in our everyday life around the world, inclusion of all countries.

Advance our space programs so space mining of non-renewable resources on the Earth can be replenished by utilizing other planets, moons and asteroids, (probably not comets). Robotics can be developed for these space mining operations and utilize our moon as a docking station. Also to meet other people from other planets for the enrichment of ourselves and other human beings.

These directives can not only stop the deterioration of planets and the Earth, but turn the deterioration around including the climates for our generation and future generations to come.

Much of the technology within the Manowar is titanium. Blind, deaf and mute, the technology was developed with titanium chips for sight, hearing and speech. This technology could possibly be developed for those who need it on all planets. Including aiding in human mobility of limbs.

The **ladder of truth** is as follows for the outlook on planets, going up for truth:

Embracement of one another as people, greatness and beauty, leadership

Acceptance of one another as people, greatness, glimmers of beauty, leadership

Indifference of one another as people, however tolerance

Non Acceptance of one another as people, hate criminals, war criminals, terrorists of humanity domestically or foreign, the offenders can be devils or people, the predominant liars of humanity, very sociopathic in nature, very toxic to most other people, even themselves, the dark evil of humanity.

Going up the **ladder of truth** leads to constructive societies and worlds, by the good holy of humanity, going down the ladder of truth leads to the destruction of societies and worlds. Having been bottomed out on the planets by the toxic people in war the people on all of the planets will now gravitate up the ladder in a constructive manner and the people on the planets can now stop the damage done to their planets and reverse the damage done to their planets for sustainability.

The Future of Our Planet in Each of Our Hands
As we take the reins,
Of the future of our planet,
And we all do our little part,
We can save both the small, and the large,
What we can each control,
Will add up to save all of the pieces,
And we bring together the whole,
For the planet's health and ours,
Just as long as the magic lasts, for all of us to stand proud
Now and for the future of all of us
As far as we can see!

GROWTH

HEAVENLY

HEALTHY

GOOD HOLY LIVING

CARING

MORE JOY LOVE HAPPINESS

GROWTH

Growth on worlds and within countries should be done the correct way, not controlled through the acts of war or hate crimes by toxic Devils or people.

Growth in societies should be done through education programs with beneficial information for all people at a very young age as well as into adulthood. These educational programs should consider the culture and religious tendencies of its population and also include the educational consideration of other cultures and religions of societies. So each person's growth should be done the correct way, always by parenting and education, including religious education.

As we grow and mature, responsibility for one's well being a priority, trust in yourself and respect for yourself as you grow are always a priority. As you grow and build relationships you have trust in yourself as you include the other involved person a similar trust and respect must also become a priority.

Hormones and pheromones are active and viable at a very young age in our population of males and females. How to express yourself with others with these active chemicals can be difficult to control and develop properly. Treating your mind, body, soul, spirit and universe as a temple as well as treating others the same can be priceless. Don't let peer pressure let you treat yourself or anyone else any less of how you would want to be treated, with trust and respect. Don't let other people exploit your considerations and don't exploit other people's considerations. When making decisions in a developing relationship always consider the outcome of the encounter and whether you are prepared for the outcome. If you are not prepared for the outcome of a sexual encounter with a partner (the possibility of a baby), prepare yourself ahead of time or avoid the sexual encounter until you are prepared. Be prepared to lean in with discussion in the course the sexual encounter is going and preparation needed for the desired outcome to happen.

Protection for birth control should be considered if the decision between two consenting partners agrees to make the decision together to have a sexual relationship. Protection should be learned by both consenting partners in educational, possibly religious and medical programs available at many community services, religious establishments and school establishments.

Some birth control protection devices are male condoms to be wore by the male, birth control pills, hormones for women, birth control pills for men, being developed, patch worn on female body per instructions, hormone, blocks egg release and blocks sperm entrance, diaphragm, for female and must be fitted by health care provider, spermicide, best used with condom, IUD intrauterine device, women, worn in the vagina, put their by health care provider, keeps sperm joining with egg, vaginal ring, female, keep the ovaries from releasing eggs, also shots for the female to halt the release of eggs. Make informed choices, these were discovered through online exploration. These are some birth control methods. All have instructions for their proper use. Many medical professionals can and will advise correctly.

Also consider protecting yourself and others from sexually transmitted diseases. Utilizing a male condom is best protection except for abstinence from a sexual encounter itself. STDs, Sexually Transmitted Diseases, Chlamydia, asymptomatic to begin with in most cases, can damage the womens reproductive system, in men swelling of the testicles and burning urination with discharge, AIDS, both male and female, Human Immunodeficiency Virus,

Papillomavirus infection, may cause warts in various parts of the body, Genital herpes, both male and female, sores. A few other STDs are Syphilis, Hepatitis, Gonorrhea, Trichomoniasis, there are many others, etc... Consult a medical professional for more information and also if a STD is suspected, consult a medical professional.

If the decision is to have a sexual relationship for child bearing, educational and medical programs are available for both consenting partners.

All communities should have educational and informative programs on partnering programs as their youth progress into adulthood and continue through adulthood for a good healthy population that is well sustained. Governments, religions and various cultures should lean into these informative programs for a healthy society. These programs should be developed and tailored for the population to support partnering at various ages of the stages of growth throughout life.

Where overcrowding is an issue in a country or world, people, genders, government and religions must lean in to manage the population in a more meaningful way for sustainability of life in the country and world. They must reach their society through health and religious educational programs in this population to control the persistence of their countries and worlds without overcrowding.

Growth in the physical infrastructure to support our human race must also keep pace for the health and well being of a society. If done with the growth of the peoples religions, genders, races and cultures can be very dynamic and exciting for all, at all ages. A two year vocational, trade, and/or college education should be available to all our young adults with government subsidies for health and well being of all people and for the proper growth of the country.

Growth through our stages of life is often done through celebrations, weddings, birth, baptism, ministries, religious celebrations in early life, recommitment of vows, anniversary celebrations, birthdays, religious holidays, country celebrations, etc. We gather, family, friends, sometimes strangers and share food and drink and merriment. These celebrations should never end. Many are commitments to our faith, family and countries and ourselves.

The **ladder of truth** is as follows in growth, going up for truth:

Embracement of one another as people, greatness and beauty, shared

Acceptance of one another as people, greatness, glimmers of beauty, shared

Indifference of one another as people, however tolerance, may be shared

Non Acceptance of one another as people, hate criminals, war criminals, terrorists of humanity domestically or foreign, the offenders can be devils or people, the predominant liars of humanity, very sociopathic in nature, very toxic to most other people, even themselves, the dark evil of humanity.

Going up the **ladder of truth** leads to constructive societies and world growth, the good holy of humanity, better health of people, families, communities, societies, worlds, happier, more harmony and balance, more productivity. Going down the ladder of truth leads to the destruction of societies and world growth.

The Truth of Growth
Growth, can start out small, can start out loud,
It is different in each one of us,
From the beginning throughout our being,
Through our eternity,
We try and grow as strong as we can, you and me,
Hopefully together, sometimes apart,
We do the best, as one within our hearts!

PEOPLE
AT A
LOSS

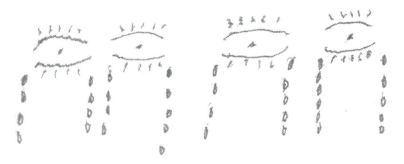

TEARS   SADNESS   DEPRESSION

ANGER   FRUSTRATION

UNCONTROLLABLE EMOTIONS

PEOPLE AT A LOSS

Loss of the war criminals the heinous terrorists of humanity that do the most harm as hate criminals by their crimes of their own doing on their planets and between planets when their crimes are all unnecessary in humanity and all unjustified and certainly not necessary for the reason of slavery and/or mental slavery, is just no excuse for these hate crimes and are a result of their own doing. Their eternal incarceration benefits all remaining living people, societies, communities, countries, governments, worlds, galaxies and universes beyond belief for the truth of law and order and justice. The criminal heinous terrorists in war exploited themselves in their loss of lifes by missing the truth of law and order and justice including freedom with their progressive offensive of humanity or offense of humanity, the dark evil of humanity, rather than join in on a progressive defense of humanity or defense of humanity, the good holy of humanity.

Losses in war can be a real hardship on families, friends and loved ones. These losses are on both the sides of war, right or wrong. To overcome the loss of life, the physical and mental maiming can take a great deal of care and time to overcome, even with professional help. It helps for the community, country and world to be empathetic to those who have suffered these great losses as they are trying to move on in their lives.

Loss and grief of people in our lives, from our loved ones, friends, relatives, and even strangers is very difficult to work through. The thought of the person no longer being involved in our future is hard to conceive and accept, at times leading to depression. For some, the same is true with pets and also important the loss of our homes, cities, and livelihoods, jobs are also losses that are hard to conceive and accept. Loss of relationships, limbs, and physical and mental capabilities are hard to conceive and accept for our future. To overcome these, the loss and grieving process is personal in each one of us, and tears are always acceptable. Family, friends, medical, counselors, and religious professionals can help us through these tragedies that happen in everyone's lives. Don't be afraid to reach out when you are ready, people will be there for you.

Sometimes once a person's life has been lost, we gather with family and friends and strangers and celebrate the lost ones life. These celebrations should never end as a celebration of their living life as well as the new beginning of their eternal life should always be allowed as well.

If the loss seems to be unmanageable, reach out to our first responders in the United States dial 911 for help. If you notice the person seems lost and unable to manage, reach out for them, dial 911 for them for help.

Penitentiary systems could be for many, much more vocational expansive in learning a trade after release. Community service could be used with good behavior and then lead to an earlier dismissal of sentence. Treatment programs for mental illness and drug and alcohol exploitations could be offered at all facilities. Behavioral treatment programs to aid with community reinstatement including reinstatement into a family setting, some for domestic inclusion. Education for high school GED and higher should be offered. Possibly offer vocational, trade, two year college certificates and four year college degrees.

Successfully, these programs would break the cycle of return offenders. Address what's missing from a person's life and they can become successful.

Lost people in the exploitation of alcohol, drugs and weapons brings not only a person out of harmony and balance, the family out of harmony and balance and the society out of harmony and balance. The loss of people is horrific with the exploitation of these vices. As well as the impact to people surrounding these people lost in these vices is an absolute hardship to deal with to watch the result of the deterioration of the person and people they affect.

Older nationals trapped in their homes. More community services could be offered to bring these older people together with others to experience a variety of indoor and outdoor adventures. They would expand their mind, body, soul, spirit and universe and other peoples also. Utilize technology to have online visits with family, relatives and friends available to all, at various times, when needed by the older adults for their consideration. Also the online technology could be for self interest educational and enlightenment experiences.

Homeless services could expand in all nations to provide adequate shelter and food for all including required medical services. A neighbor once told me everyone deserves a vacation. Did he mean everyone, could you imagine! Remember, even adequate temporary toilet facilities and temporary cleansing facilities at these temporary mobile homeless camps can go a long way until the homeless can be placed, educated, trained and achieve work functionality.

People with the losses of food and water resources (the hungry), whether they have a home or not, must be served and protected and provided with food and water resources for pure humanitarian reasons in all communities, countries in all worlds on an ongoing basis, never to end, it's the Good/Holy in almost all of us.

The **ladder of truth** is as follows in peoples loss, going up for truth:

Embracement of one another as people, greatness and beauty, great aid

Acceptance of one another as people, greatness, glimmers of beauty, aid

Indifference of one another as people, however tolerance

Non Acceptance of one another as people, hate criminals, war criminals, terrorists of humanity domestically or foreign, the offenders can be devils or people, the predominant liars of humanity, very sociopathic in nature, very toxic to most other people, even themselves, the dark evil of humanity.

Going up the **ladder of truth** leads to constructive societies and worlds in people's losses, the good holy of humanity, helping each other through losses, going down the ladder of truth leads to the destruction of societies and worlds in people's losses. The casualties in war will be kept to a bare minimum as the toxic offenders will not be able to perpetuate war or slavery, they will no longer be allowed to bring the rest of society down to their toxic level and be destroyed.

Embracement
When we reach out to the people who need it the most,
The feeling inside light, within us,
If we can bring a spark of fire, and peace to a moment of life,
It may make a person's whole entire day,
To sit isolated in a dismal situation, is not a nice way,
Bringing a smile and some conversation,
May make a huge difference,
In just an unbelievable way!

PASSION
OF
CHRIST

PASSION
IN
YOU

COVENANTS

VALUES

VIRTUES

PASSION OF CHRIST

The Passion of the Lord God Almighty and the Passion of Jesus is the Passion of Christ, sealed as Father and Son, part of the passion is to try and carry humanities sins through the suffrage of both in the crucifiction of Jesus, before, during and after the crucifiction. The Passion of Christ is carried through even today as it always will be. Another part of the Passion of Christ is for people to lead a good holy life as they can throughout a person's lifetime, while being forgiven for their sins of living. Part of the Passion of Christ is to bring out the real Passion of You, the best in you as a human being. And there is more...

The Covenant contains the Lord God Almighty, Jesus, the Passion of Christ and Holy Spirits including the Beast (part of the pond of redemption) and their availability to all humanity.

With this new launching point on Earth and all the Lord God Almighty planets, a new buzz is being renewed for the Passion of the Lord God Almighty, Passion of Jesus and Passion of Christ, Passion of the Covenant, and the Passion of You. These buzz's will spread like wildfire, uncontainable amongst We The People as we stand united.

Religious writings of old will be brought up to date in today's world, not lost but updated to be more relevant by all religions on all the Lord God Almighty planets including the Earth by each religious organization, including certain religious celebrations. They will bring out how you fit into the family, community, country, world, and universe in our changing environment. This will reduce stress, reduce fear, help keep the peace and help keep people free. Religious writings of old will not be lost, but taught, and kept for all times.

To guard, protect and serve the Lord God Almighty, Jesus, Christ, Holy Spirits, the flocks of the Lord God Almighty the Lord wrote a prophecy that a Manowar would be called to stand for all said in protection of the Lords flocks from the horrors of war, the Devils vessel, the Arc of Covenant, which includes the horrors of slavery and/or mental slavery. This is part of the Passion of the Manowar and never double indemnity of the Lord God Almighty or his flocks in this honor, service and duty to the Lord God Almighty and his flocks. This protection is not only mandated by the Lord God Almighty, but required for all humanity to protect the Lord God Almighty flocks of self rights and entitlements that were given at the beginning, Peace and Freedom. The Manowar is at the apex of the cross when the sign of the cross is made, shared with the Lord God Almighty to become the other half of He, to save humanity, from the Devils and humanities own destruction of domestic and foreign terrorism to lead all to Peace and Freedom.

The Manowar is also the Arch-Angel of Tough Love and protects the Cross and Covenant of the Passion of Christ for all people, the gifts for humanity, Love, Compassion, Faith, Grace, Mercy, and Forgiveness and more to be available for all humanity.

The Manowar in the dimensions of his mind, body, soul, spirit and universe and with the Beast descended on him in the dimension of his mind, body, soul, spirit, and universe reached up to heaven and with the hand of the Lord God Almighty added the progressive protection and defense including justice of humanity from the progressive offense and offensive of humanity in war and added the laws and rules to the Covenant itself as well as the enforcement laws and rules and due process rules of the engagement in war itself for Peace and Freedom. As humanity could not achieve this same goal with a offense or progressive offense, rather life in the horrors of war and ultimately the end of all life on their planets, this progressive protection and defense had to come from the Lord God Almighty, the Beast and the Manowar for all humanity on all of the Lord God Almighty planets and was so mandated. We have no guilt in this progressive protection and defense of all humanity. All are free to join in on this protection and defense of all humanity and this protection. As a matter of fact this progressive defense is the wish of the preponderance of all humanity. Written in prophecy towards the beginning of time to happen when needed. An added gift and blessing for humanity, to hold the cross, the Covenants together for all humanity now and all humanity to come. With this reach up to heaven with the Lord God Almighty hand, the Vortex of Protection was built and perfected, as the Manowar, the Vortex of Repairation and a Vortex of Retribution was built as well. The Vortex of Repairation can be modified further to aid in humanities health. The Manowar could not figure out how to populate the Vortex of Retribution for any and all of humanity, little is in it.

With these being built the four Horsemen and the Prophecy itself are part of the Covenant themselfs, the Lord God Almighty, Jesus, Holy Spirits (including the Beast) men and women, Manowar in the venture of the Protection and the Reparation of humanity.

The Laws and Rules of the engagement in war include the laws and rules to protect and defend all humanity and worlds from the criminal offenders in war above all humanities laws and rules, governments laws and rules and courts of laws and rules, including at the planet level, the due process to administer the laws and rules and to execute the laws and rules to each and every person in humanity and were added into the Covenant for Gifts and Blessings to all humanity as a progressive defense in all wars. As part of the Gift of the Covenant as being given the second chance at life at becoming someone other than a war criminal, a hate criminal, possibly even becoming someone other than a hate criminal in society is priceless.

The Covenant of the Cross, the Passion of Christ not only contains the Love, Compassion, Grace, Mercy, Hope, and Forgiveness it contains, each person's self right and entitlement for Peace and

Freedom, it contains the dimensions of a person's mind, body, soul, spirit and universe and the self right and entitlement to Worship, have Faith, and believe in the Passion of Christ and the Covenant itself. The Covenant contains the laws and rules for all humanity to live by and be defended by for the truth, laws and rules of the Ten Commandments, contains many vows, such as ministry and clergy, baptism, wedding, funerary, places to Worship, Adornment, The Cross Itself, Holy water the Sacraments, Eucharist, Holy Blood of Christ, Holy Body of Christ, Holy Rites, Holy Places as they relate to religions. It contains each person's right to express their emotions as needed in all of life's situations. This includes the Covenant experience of music, dance, songs and ceremonies. This includes art, artwork and the expression of art form. There is more to the Covenant than listed here. The symbol of the Body of Christ itself, as well as the Body of Christ itself. The Covenant contains the virtues and values available to humanity, some are listed in the Passion of You chapter. All in the Covenant Blessings for humanity, Gifts for humanity, the Blessings, part of the Covenant itself.

Often beauty is brought before the congregation in the celebration of the Passion of Christ, to be shown and respected, the reverence, to be brought home and shared and spread amongst each other. Often this joy and beauty is spread at religious and other holidays throughout the year. Also this joy and beauty is spread through our hearts through volunteerism, evangelism and giving careers.

The part of the Passion of Christ that is available to all living people is to lean in on Christ during the growth of a person's life in happiness and tribulations in everyday life as well as ceremonies. With that said, the same is true for the Passion of Christ to be available to all living people during everyday lives, including thankfulness for food and drink. Also the Passion of Christ to be available to people with losses and grief in their lives, as well as ceremonies. With this the Passion of Christ and the people religions can conform and live in a harmony and balance with the dimensions of their lives with their mind, body, soul, spirit and universe.

The Passion of Christ brings a great deal of empathy to one another and much more to us in our times of trials and tribulations. The divine power of Christ will believe in you and have faith in you to know right from wrong and will give you strength to follow the right path through life. This will allow you the mindfulness to see the beauty within Them, within You, as well as the beauty within Others.

Part of the Passion of Christ is forgiveness for mistakes gone array in our lives. Some humans have this forgiveness in them and some do not. Not everything can be forgiven, but the preponderance of mistakes are forgiven with the Passion of Christ. In many religions this is the pond of redemption, where the sins are washed and cleansed. If you can forgive yourself, maybe its easier to forgive others!

The **ladder of truth** in for the Passion of Christ is as follows, going up for truth:

Embracement of one another as people, greatness and beauty, more heavenly

Acceptance of one another as people, greatness, also more heavenly, glimmers of beauty

Indifference of one another as people, however tolerance, more likely heavenly

Non Acceptance of one another as people, hate criminals, war criminals, terrorists of humanity domestically or foreignly, the offenders can be devils or people, the predominant liars of humanity, very sociopathic in nature, more harmful that leads to soul/spirit and aura repairation in purgatory or even possible the worst outcome Hell, the dark evil of humanity.

More people will be going up the **ladder of truth** leading to constructive societies, the good holy of humanity, more forgiving families, communities, countries and worlds with the Passion of

Christ, rather than going down the ladder of truth leading to the destruction of societies and worlds. This would lead to a person gravitating in a heavenly direction. The toxic people that refused to end their war or slave mastery would have their lives ended and would be war prisoners in purgatory or Hell, the dark evil of humanity, they could not find the key to the Covenant. The rest of humanity would naturally gravitate up the ladder in life and afterlife, the good holy of humanity, as they found the key to the truth and Covenant.

Not all religions are exactly Christianity, however, based on many similarities and many of the same truths.

Passion of Christ and You
The Passion of Christ in You, was always meant to be shared,
With family, friends, relatives, strangers, and volunteers,
At church, with faith, with meaning, where people care,
At work, play, meals, leisure time,
With the god given tools,
And appreciation for life,
Helping yourself and others, each and every moment,
All along the way we wonder,
And we know that this is the right path for me!

Passion of Christ
The Passion of Christ is a lean from above,
Its at a time of loss and sorrow,
A time of enjoyment, happiness and celebration,
It can be at a time of solace,
A time of calm,
It can be by yourself, shared with a few or many,
It can be done quietly, or loudly,
As Christ hears our shout's,
We listen, and give him our questions,
He answers,
And our minds dance more clearly all about and about!

PASSION
IN
YOU

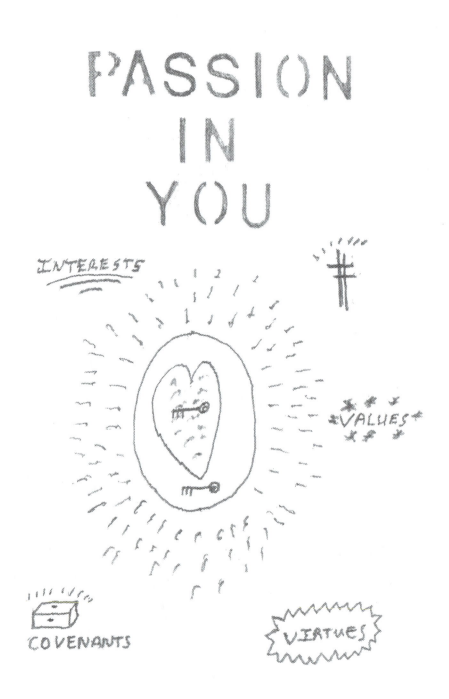

INTERESTS

VALUES

COVENANTS

VIRTUES

PASSION IN YOU

What is the passion in you? Your personal goals, family goals, career goals? What is the fire that will bring your Peace and Freedom in life to achieve these?

If the Passion in You is to find a significant other, look for another with similar religious beliefs, virtues and values, possibly similar tastes, some similar interests to be your matching bookend. Be truthful to yourself and each other, it goes a long way.

Bring the Passion of Christ into your life with the Covenants to help hold together your life and bind you and your family and friends. Part of the Covenant, Worship, Love, Compassion, Faith, Grace, Mercy, Hope and Forgiveness and more...

What are virtues in you that help define you, there are many, like honesty, courage, vision, compassion, care, fairness, strive for excellence, creativeness, sensitivity, empathy, generosity, integrity, prudence, justice and fortitude, the quality of being morally good, tranquility, humility, moderation, cleanliness, protection of humanities exploitations, and more..., too many to list...

What are values that help define you like merit, worth, usefulness, practicality, advantage, desirability, benefit, advantage, gain, profit, service, help, helpfulness, assistance, effectiveness, efficacy, importance, significance, principles, ethics, morals, standards, many many more, too many to list...

With these Covenants, virtues and values how can you leverage them to lead to your interests in life, like public speaking, government service, ministries, teaching, doctoring, nursing, counseling, child care, adult care, construction, law enforcement, defense, transportation, power and service industry, landscaping, plant nursery, sports of all kinds, table games, yard games, volunteerism, evangelism, church socials, music, dance, art, walks, jogging, pet care, gardening of various kinds, lawn care, hobbies, like : knitting, coin collecting, stamp collecting, many many others, too many to list...

The Passion of Christ, Covenant, virtues, values and interests lead to accepting each other and a balanced and harmonious life in society.

Some people know what these goals are for themself for the dimension of their mind, body, soul, spirit, and universe, some don't. Either case, it doesn't hurt to communicate with your family, relatives and in most cases your friends these goals. It can even help to bounce these goals off of career and/or guidance counselors, religious counselors and professionals in the industry you are thinking about advancing your life towards. Leaning into the Passion of Christ will help you through life and your religious leaders who also lean into You and the Passion of Christ. Each individual is different, like the many many stars, soon you may realize the Passion of You and maybe the meaning of life to you. It's to believe in yourself and the Passion of Christ to give you the strength to follow your chosen direction/ dream and stick to it. It's the faith that the Passion of Christ can be there for you when called upon that is a difference maker. Be true to yourself and fight for the truth, you will come out way ahead in life's Covenants, virtues and values and interests. More opportunities will arise with these types of Covenants, virtues and values instilled in you. The energy in the beauty of the Passion of Christ will bring out the energy in the beauty in the Passion of You. Once this energy and beauty is instilled in you, it will be spread to others around you.

If you're just starting out looking for a career or looking for a career change, or a change in life, attitude within can often lead to your ultimate success. Be positive, creative, strong, a bit enthusiastic and willing to go the extra mile.

If you're a gang member, is your passion, crimes, hate crimes and violence to reach prison for self fulfillment and pleasure for yourself, family and career? Or can you alter your attitude to reach a more fulfilling life for yourself, family and career? Can you reach out to the right people who have the passion within them to help you with your passion? They are out there!

How do you alter your attitude? It's within you. List out your personal, family and career goals. Gravitate to others who are successfully reaching their goals. Gravitate to other peers and educational and vocational and religious professionals that have a positive outlook for the goals you would like to achieve. With the right attitude, positive outlook, and drive you can achieve your goals! You may have to consult a guidance counselor and take a self interest test to see where others with similar interests have found fulfilling careers. Consult job counselors to help you acquire a job.

Part of the Passion of You should be to defend our law and order system to protect people from harm. Side with the proper authorities in this venture. If you are stopped by law enforcement officers, don't run, don't fight, don't flight. Stay calm, listen and respond responsibly and with respect. In all likelihood the outcome will be mutual and peaceful and the ending will be harmless!

Part of the Passion in You should be found in nature. If you can even get out for a day event in parks or on lakes, streams and oceans and they can really lift your spirit and lift the spirits of those you are enjoying the experience with.

Part of the Passion in You should be not to exploit other peoples races, religions, cultures and genders. Try not to exploit alcohol, illegal and legal drugs. If you can manage the exploitation of yourself and the exploitation of others, you can lead a very satisfying life.

Part of the Passion in You should be to reach your dimension of the mind, body, soul, spirit, and universe. Reach the Passion of Christ and the Covenant and defend the pieces contained in the

Covenant, virtues and values as best you can as a person, family, community and country, possibly even at a world level.

Part of the Passion in You should be to accept the Passion of Christ, the reverence and Covenant and pass this along to others. Explore the Passion of Christ for the religion you were born into, this can be very self fulfilling. Sometimes education classes are offered or materials to help you with this venture. Find the best religion of the Passion of Christ for your faith if the one you were born into does not suit you. For enlightenment it helps to explore other religions and cultures of humanity. This can bring a more togetherness of societies.

With finding the Covenant of the Passion of Christ, the dimensions you can attain in your mind, body, soul, spirit, and universe and the values, virtues and interests in you and significant people in your life you will find the Passion in You and come to grips with more of a meaning of your life!

The **ladder of truth** is as follows for the Passion of You, going up for truth:

Embracement of one another as people, greatness and beauty, great leaders

Acceptance of one another as people, greatness, glimmers of beauty, leaders

Indifference of one another as people, however tolerance

Non Acceptance of one another as people, hate criminals, war criminals, terrorists of humanity domestically or foreign, the offenders can be devils or people, the predominant liars of humanity, very sociopathic in nature, very toxic to most other people, even themselves, the dark evil of humanity.

Going up the **ladder of truth** leads to constructive societies and worlds including the Passion of You, the good holy of humanity, reaching dreams, going down the ladder of truth leads to the destruction of societies and worlds including the destruction of the potential of the Passion of You. With the Passion of You always try to gravitate up the ladder and avoid being a toxic person in war or a toxic person in Peace and Freedom, as well as society to lead a Good Holy life, the key to the Covenant, virtues, values, interests and key to yourself.

Be someone, up the ladder of truth, for yourself and others, CARE, the Lord God Almighty, Jesus, Passion of Christ, Beast, Holy Spirits, Manowar, your family, people up the ladder of truth, absolutely CARE.

This can work for anybody!

Passion In You
How do I fit
In this huge big space,
I feel a bit awkward,
A bit out of place,
With inner Peace and Freedom,
Family, relatives, some friends, and with some guidance,
I will get along in this world much better, and actually great,
I will do this with all my fight, and all
my might, and a bit of grace!

PERSONAL
DIRECTION

PERSONAL DIRECTION

Printed in the United States
by Baker & Taylor Publisher Services